HOW PHILOSOPHY BEGINS

The Aquinas Lecture, 1983

HOW PHILOSOPHY BEGINS

Under the auspices of the
Wisconsin-Alpha Chapter of Phi Sigma Tau

by
BEATRICE H. ZEDLER

MARQUETTE UNIVERSITY PRESS
MILWAUKEE
1983

Library of Congress Catalogue Card Number: 82-63007

© Copyright 1983
Marquette University

ISBN 0-87462-151-8

Dedicated to the memory of my parents
Edwin and Cecelia Zedler:
my first teachers

Prefatory

The Wisconsin-Alpha Chapter of Phi Sigma Tau, the National Honor Society for Philosophy at Marquette University, each year invites a scholar to deliver a lecture in honor of St. Thomas Aquinas.

The 1983 Aquinas Lecture *How Philosophy Begins* was delivered in the Todd Wehr Chemistry Building on Sunday, February 27, 1983, by Beatrice H. Zedler, Professor of Philosophy at Marquette University.

After receiving her B.A. from Marquette University *summa cum laude,* Dr. Zedler also earned an M.A. from Marquette and a Ph.D. from Fordham University, Bronx, New York. She taught at Marian College, Fond du Lac, Wisconsin, and at College Misericordia, Dallas, Pennsylvania, before returning to Marquette University in 1946 where she became Professor of Philosophy in 1963. Dr. Zedler was twice appointed to the Marquette University Women's Chair of Humanistic Studies and in 1981 received the Faculty Award for Teaching Excellence.

Dr. Zedler edited *Averroes' Destructio Destructionum Philosophiae Algazelis* (1961) and translated and edited St. Thomas Aquinas' *On the Unity of the Intellect against the Averroists* (1968); she has also edited two volumes of essays by Gerard Smith, S.J., *Christian Philosophy and its Future* (1971) and *A Trio of Talks* (1971). Her articles on Christian and Islamic philosophy in the Middle Ages and on American philosophy have appeared in the *New Catholic Encyclopedia,* in books, and in journals. Dr. Zedler is a member of the American Catholic Philosophical Association, the American Philosophical Association, and the Medieval Academy of America.

Professor's Zedler's scholarly work — whether on Averroes, Avicenna, and Aquinas or on John Dewey and William James — has been esteemed by her peers; her teaching has been appreciated by both graduate and undergraduate students during her many years at Marquette.

To Dr. Zedler's distinguished list of publications Phi Sigma Tau is pleased to add: *How Philosophy Begins*.

Foreword

Father Gerard Smith, S.J., who was chairman of the Marquette Philosophy Department for twenty-two years, used to say that the Aquinas Lectures helped to push back the frontiers of ignorance. And, indeed, many of the previous speakers in this series have done just that, with a clarity and brilliance of insight that have illumined the minds of other philosophers on specialized topics. My remarks will be a more modest attempt.

As a teacher who has tried to explain some difficult concepts, I have often been aware of some questions in the minds of my students, such questions, for example, as these: "To whom are you speaking, professor? Will you please speak to *us*? If you must talk philosophy, can you lead us into it gently? Can you show us how and why philosophy begins?"

It is these questions that I should like to address. For my professional colleagues this lecture may serve as a souvenir of a journey begun long ago. For students it may serve as a passport to a journey that they just now are beginning.

How Philosophy Begins

The word *philosopher* means lover of wisdom, but not all philosophers have lived up to their name. Sometimes they have not been loving, and sometimes they have not been wise.

They seem to be involved in perpetual controversy without getting anything settled. Nominalists fight realists; pluralists fight monists; determinists fight free-willists. In commenting on philosophers, one writer has said: "Prolixity is their manner and their disputes are too many."[1]

Philosophers are seen not only as disputatious but also as out of touch with reality. Who can forget the story of the maid-servant laughing at Thales when he fell into a ditch as he was looking up at the stars? He was so eager to know what was going on in the heavens, she said, that he could not see what was at his feet.[2] And Louisa May Alcott, thinking of her Transcendentalist father, Bronson Alcott, defined a philosopher as "a man up in a balloon, with his family and friends holding the ropes which confine him to earth and trying to haul him down."[3]

Philosophers often use abstract terms remote from everyday language, for example: analogy of proper proportionality, transcendental analytic, concrescence, entelechy, haecceity. One is reminded of the dialogue in Gilbert and Sullivan's *Princess Ida.* When the Princess asks: "Who lectures in the Hall of Arts today?" Blanche responds:

> I, madam, on Abstract Philosophy.
> There I propose considering at length,
> Three points — The Is, the Might Be, and the Must.
> Whether the Is, from being actual fact,
> Is more important than the vague Might Be,
> Or the Might Be, from taking wider scope,
> Is for that reason greater than the Is;
> And lastly, how the Is and Might Be stand
> Compared with the inevitable Must![4]

To this the Princess says: "The subject's deep."

One might well ask: Why bother with philosophy? Why not ignore the disputes and the bloodless abstractions of philosophers and leave philosophy alone?

The fact is that we can't avoid philosophy. Everyone has a philosophy, whether or not that philosophy has been explicitly formulated. Each person's thoughts and actions imply some view of the nature of reality, of the human person, of the purpose of life. Some may spend little time in reflection because of the pressures of daily tasks and the distractions of pleasant recreation, but sooner or later everyone seeks some understanding of his or her experience.

I. Philosophy Begins in Wonder

Many centuries ago Aristotle pointed out that all men by nature desire to know. When almost all the necessities of life had been provided and the things that make for comfort and recreation had been secured, then knowledge for the sake of understanding began to be sought. Aristotle says: "It is owing to their wonder that men both now begin and at first began to philosophize."[5] And before him Plato had said: "Wonder is the feeling of a philosopher and philosophy begins in wonder."[6]

This wonder of which Plato and Aristotle speak can be seen even in young children. They ask more questions than their elders can answer. Why does it get dark at night? How does a seed know what kind of a plant to grow into? Why do skinless wieners have skins on? As we grow older, the content of our questions may change, but we still wonder. We might wonder, for example: Who am I? What am I?

Why am I here? Is there any meaning or purpose to my existence? How can I make right choices? Has this world in which I find myself always existed or did it have a beginning in time? Is there a God? Why does something exist rather than nothing?

We might pause for a few moments to wonder about wonder. What is this wonder with which philosophy begins? It is apparently a human reaction to something, but what is the something that is the occasion for wonder? What is wonder itself? What is its connection with knowing?

A *res mira,* a wonder, could be something astonishing; it could be a *miraculum,* a miracle like the raising of a man from the dead which is beyond the power of created nature.[7] Or it could be a natural phenomenon: birth, growth, the continuous sequence of day and night, the change of seasons. It could be something surprising, shocking, or simply new and different in human experience: something that interrupts the previous pattern of a human life, such as falling in love, a sudden misfortune, a serious illness, the death of a close relative or friend.[8] It could be a situation which requires a choice or what Dewey calls a forked-road situation: a situation which halts the smooth gliding of our activity by presenting a dilemma, which proposes alternatives.[9] It could be an intellectual challenge in which, as William James describes it, some new facts or new ideas jostle against our old stock of opinions and create an inward trouble.[10]

But that something which is the occasion for wonder need not force itself upon our consciousness; it need not come as an intruder. It can be a simple thing to which we quietly give our attention. In the busy-ness of our adult lives, we may do this less often than children. Some of the simple objects of a child's wonder are mentioned in a poem written by a mother who also happened to be the wife of a philosopher. The poem, inspired by her three-year-old son, is called "The Eyes of Wonder":

> All things are wonderful to him
> > Who is but lately three;
> Still guided by the seraphim
> He steps upon the earth's bright rim,
> > Nor parts with heaven's key.
>
> He walks among created things
> > With unperverted sight;
> And all the birds have golden wings,
> And sticks and stones are made for kings
> > To handle with delight.
>
> And I, who shall see ten times three
> > No longer and no more,
> Am sometimes privileged to see,
> To look where I shall never be,
> > Behind that hidden door.[11]

All things can be an occasion for wonder: birds, sticks, stones, and, we might add, flowers, recalling how Tennyson plucked a flower from the crannied wall and reflected, as he held it in his hand:

Little flower—but *if* I could understand
What you are, root and all, and all in all,
I should know what God and man is.[12]

Not only this or that individual thing but the manyness of things can be a source of wonder, for we seem to inhabit not a multiverse, but a universe. Since the time of the Pre-Socratics people have wondered about a principle of unity amid the plurality of existing things. Do all things come from water? Do all things come from air? Do all things come from fire?

Almost anything, as we have suggested, can be an occasion for wonder. But what is wonder itself? It seems to be an emotive reaction to something we are aware of. In the presence of something that surpasses our human power of comprehension, it can take the form of awe. Perhaps it was this sort of wonder that Augustine and his mother Monica felt when, as they stood at the window at Ostia, quietly talking about eternal life, they seemed to go beyond their own minds; it seemed to them that if all things were hushed, they might hear God's very self and touch eternal wisdom.[13]

In moments when wonder is awe, there is "a pause of reason." The intellect may be silent. Describing such moments, William James said: ". . . the intellect itself is hushed to sleep . . . . Ontological emotion so fills the soul that ontological speculation can no longer overlap it and put her girdle of interrogation-marks round existence."[14] But, in many other experiences of wonder, as Samuel Johnson said: "The awful stillness of attention with which the mind is overspread at the first view of an unexpected effect, ceases when we have leisure to disentangle complications and investigate causes."[15] What begins as a wondering *at* may become a wondering *why*.[16]

This is implied in some of St. Thomas' comments on how wonder arises and what wonder is. Thomas Aquinas, like Aristotle, thinks that wonder is what leads us to philosophy.[17] Aristotle had said that one who is puzzled and wonders thinks himself ignorant and philosophizes in order to escape from ignorance, and St. Thomas agrees.[18] We wonder about that of whose cause we are ignorant. If we already knew the cause, we would not wonder. [19] The effect might be above nature, beyond the operation of nature, or contrary to the course of nature and produced immediately by divine power, and, in any of these instances, the cause of which we are ignorant might be hidden in itself, hidden absolutely. But often the cause of an effect that we are trying to understand is not beyond the power of nature or beyond the ability of the human mind to grasp. It is not hidden absolutely but only to this or that person. [20] In either case, the wonder that we feel is a kind of fear.

According to Thomas, wonder is a species of fear following upon the apprehension of something exceeding our knowledge and sometimes exceeding our ability to know it. [21] Fear, in his context, is one of the irascible passions which have as their object something seen as difficult. The object of fear is a difficult evil not yet avoided and not easily avoided. [22]

Sometimes, though not always, wonder may be a reaction to something perceived as a great evil event (for example, a devastating earthquake, a volcanic eruption, a hurricane), but whether the occasion for wonder be something good or evil, there is an aspect of difficulty here, the difficulty of considering a great and unusual thing. [23]

It is not just that we fear the hardship involved in trying to comprehend something that seems beyond our grasp, but we fear remaining in ignorance. This ignorance *(ignorantia)* is not a *nescientia;* it is not total absence of knowledge, but a lack of knowledge of something we ought to know.[24] We must be aware of our ignorance in order to fear and dislike it.

But why do we fear and dislike it? Since the proper operation of man as man is to understand, our desire for understanding does not allow us to be satisfied with just having an awareness of some effect. Explicitly relating this to wonder, Thomas says: ". . . there resides in every man a natural desire to know the cause of any effect which he sees. Thence arises wonder in man." And elsewhere he adds that "wonder is a certain desire for knowing."[25]

That Thomas in some texts speaks of wonder as a species of fear, an irascible passion, and in others, links it to desire, a concupiscible passion, is not contradictory. The passions of the irascible appetite (which have as their object something seen as difficult to obtain or avoid) arise from and terminate in passions of the concupiscible appetite (which have as their object something seen as easy or simple to obtain or avoid). Fear and desire are therefore related.

Fear is concerned with an avoidance of an evil, but the avoidance of an evil arises from a desire for a good.[26] "There is no cause of fear," says Thomas, "except that a loved good may be lost."[27] It is because we desire to know truth that we fear ignorance. Thus wonder involves both fear and desire and, indeed, says St. Thomas, wonder is also a cause of delight insofar as it includes hope of attaining knowledge of that which we desire to know.[28]

The reason why we can wonder at all is that we are knowing beings, but what does this mean? What is the cognitive context in which wonder occurs? When we wonder, we wonder about something. We have an awareness of something: an openness to the real. If we were non-knowing beings, we would be limited, restricted to being just what we are and nothing more. We would be closed in upon ourselves like a stone, an iron nail, a wooden lectern. Each of these is what it is and nothing more. But we as knowing beings are ourselves and yet are open to all other beings as well. Thomas says that the soul is "in a certain way all things" *(quodammodo omnia)*.[29] His meaning is not that the knower is physically transformed into the things that it knows, or that things are physically changed into the knower. You may remember the old limerick that says:

There was a young lady from Niger
Who smiled as she rode on a tiger.
   They came back from the ride
   With the lady inside
And the smile on the face of the tiger.[30]

The last two lines imply that a drastic physical assimilation has occurred, but a cognitive union is quite different.

St. Thomas teaches that the knower in knowing becomes things in an immaterial way, and things become the knower insofar as, being known, they exist in the knower in an immaterial way.[31] It is this kind of becoming that is implied in these lines from Walt Whitman:

There was a child went forth every day
And the first object he look'd upon,
   that object he became.
And that object became part of him.
. . . .
The early lilacs became part of this child
And grass and white and red morning glories
   and white and red clover,
   and the song of the phoebe-bird.[32]

As knowing beings, we, like that child, are open to the things we encounter. They become part of us insofar as they come to exist in us immaterially in a knowledge way, or, as philosophers would say, "with an intentional mode of existence."

We first encounter the world of material things by way of our senses. Within the data that reach us by way of our senses our mind discerns *what* a thing is and is thereby enabled to form a concept. When we affirm or deny that the object of the concept *is* or is connected with or is identical with the object of another concept, we not only know but we know that we know. We are then making a judgment. That judgment will be true if our thought conforms to reality.[33]

But sometimes what is given in our sense images, concepts, and judgments is astonishing, surprising; its explanation is hidden from us. And sometimes one carefully reached judgment seems incompatible with another. The wonder aroused by such experiences stimulates discursive thought by which our mind tries to move step by step towards understanding. Thus it is from our experience of the known real that the philosophic search begins.[34]

Let us look at this more closely. So far we have seen, mainly on a theoretical level, what is meant by saying that philosophy begins in wonder about something we are aware of in our own experience. Now, by looking at examples from the lives of some philosophers, we shall try to see more concretely how philosophy begins.

Following that, we shall consider the philosophical basis for how philosophy begins, that is, its basis in our human nature.

II. Examples of How Philosophy Begins

Etienne Gilson has remarked that the biography of a philosopher, while it cannot wholly account for philosophical events, is of great help in understanding a person's philosophy.[35] And Anton Pegis has noted that "all genuine philosophies are personal, however much they aim to be universal and objective in their vision."[36]

To look at the personal aspect of a philosophy, at the experiences in a person's life that aroused wonder, is to see how an individual's philosophy begins. It also helps to dispel the impression that philosophy is nothing but a set of abstractions having no connection with everyday life. Montaigne once noted that some people have given philosophy a bad image. They have represented it as "a thing of difficult access, . . . with a grim and formidable aspect." He says they have "placed it upon a rock apart, among thorns and brambles, and made of it a hobgoblin to affright people."[37]

We shall not try to show that no man's philosophy has been caught among thorns and

brambles, but only that not all philosophy must
be grim and formidable and difficult of access.
A biographical approach to the study of philosophers, while not explaining everything, may
provide some access to their thought. We cannot here re-tell the whole history of philosophy
or even the whole history of a philosopher, but
we shall recall some significant episodes from
philosophers' lives — briefly for several of them;
more fully for the thinker whom we honor in
this lecture series. This may show concretely
how wonder has led to philosophical reflection.

Sometimes suffering or even imminent
death precipitates philosophical thinking. As
Samuel Johnson once said: "Depend upon it,
Sir, when a man knows he is to be hanged in a
fortnight, it concentrates his mind
wonderfully."[38]

Recalling a famous philosophical context,
we may think of Socrates' last day and the
serious questions that he and his friends
discussed during those hours before sundown.
For many years prior to that he had, of course,
taught his followers to lead examined lives, and
now as they sat with him in prison, awaiting
the time when the jailer would bring the hem-
lock, it was natural to wonder whether or not
the soul would die with the body. The

approaching death of Socrates provides the occasion for him and his friends to examine the question of the immortality of the soul.[39]

Some four hundred years later young Epictetus was sold into slavery by his parents. He had a cruel master who, according to legend, may have twisted and broken the leg of his slave. From the troubles of his life Epictetus developed a Stoic philosophy that helped him to survive and endure many hardships. Anticipating the modern "serenity prayer," he gave some advice on what we should do when something harsh and difficult confronts us. We should ask whether it is or is not in our power to do something about it. If it is not in our power, we should be ready to say it is nothing to us. He thinks that "men are disturbed not by things but by the view which they take of things."[40] From his own experience he learned that if we cannot change the outward circumstance, we can at least change our attitude towards it; for that *is* in our power.

In the early part of the sixth century Boethius, who held a high position at the court of Theodoric, king of the Ostrogoths, was unjustly accused of treason, imprisoned in a dungeon, and eventually executed on orders of the king. The year of imprisonment which preceded his death gave him the time to wonder about happiness, evil, and providence. He recorded his reflections in a work entitled *The Consolation of Philosophy*. Here Philosophy is personified as a noble lady who gives him some answers to his difficult questions. [41]

In the eleventh and twelfth centuries some professional and personal calamities caused Abelard to reflect. In his *Historia Calamitatum* Abelard tells how, as a brilliant, arrogant, aggressive scholar, he had delighted in sharply criticizing such respected thinkers of his time as William of Champeaux and Anselm of Laon, but after he became famous, one of his most cherished treatises was condemned and burned. [42] He also tells how, while serving as tutor to Heloise, the niece of Canon Fulbert, he had seduced her, and later was castrated at the order of the angry uncle. [43] Wondering why he had to endure these and other troubles, he concludes that God wished to provide a cure for his lechery and his pride in his learning. [44] For both Boethius and Abelard the shock of a sudden reversal of fortune led to a reflection on providence.

Sometimes a simple and less critical type of experience has raised questions that have led to philosophical thinking. When Augustine at the age of sixteen stole some pears with his friends, he wondered why he had done so. He was aware that theft was wrong. He was not hungry. The pears were not good, and after he had picked them, he threw them away. In trying to understand his act of stealing, he considered various explanations of why people do wrong. This was the first of his many reflections on the cause and nature of moral evil.[45]

In the early seventeenth century a French schoolboy's experience of mathematics was to affect his philosophical thinking. When the young René Descartes attended the Jesuit school of La Flèche, he was disappointed in philosophy because though it had been studied for centuries, nothing seemed to be settled. As for ethics, he compared the moral writings of the ancient pagans "to proud and magnificent palaces that are built on nothing but sand and mud."[46] When at the end of his formal schooling, he found that he had many doubts and wondered how to resolve them, his remembrance of another school subject provided the clue. Mathematics had pleased him because of the certainty and evidence of its arguments. Its practical application had been stressed by his teacher, but René was astonished that no one had built anything more noble on its firm and

solid foundations. His encounter with mathematics at school was to lead him to give the
mathematical method a central place in his
philosophical thinking.[47]

Even more than most philosophers Søren
Kierkegaard turned his experiences into reflection. The famous three stages, that is, the
aesthetic stage in which there is no self-
commitment, the ethical stage in which subor-
dination to moral law is chosen, and the religious stage which is marked by a leap of faith, are
sometimes seen as a universalizing of his personal experience.[48] As a young man Kierkegaard
lived for a time a life of pleasure. Then after
seeing the either/or (that is, the restless aesthetic life which leads to despair *or* the resolute
commitment of the self to duty, as exemplified
in the constancy of marriage), he became
engaged. But for him the ethical stage was not
the final stage; beyond it he saw the religious
stage in which man is called to a faith like that
of Abraham. Kierkegaard may have regarded
himself as moving from the ethical stage to being a man of absolute religious commitment
when he broke his engagement to Regina
Olsen, despite the fact that he loved her and
had wanted to marry and have a home and
family.[49] Many men have broken engage-

ments, yet few philosophers have reflected on the subject as fully as he has done. But, as one historian has rightly remarked, for Kierkegaard, "philosophy and biography go together."[50]

Gabriel Marcel once said that there can be no apprehension of reality which is not accompanied by a certain shock.[51] In his *Essay in Autobiography* he tells of a shock he experienced in World War I that affected his philosophical thought and explains "the change of tone and key" that is noticeable in the second part of his *Metaphysical Journal.* In August 1914 he had been asked to serve as the head of the information service organized by the Red Cross. His office was besieged with inquiries about missing soldiers, and, in the majority of cases, the news he had to report was the news of their death. Every day he received personal visits from unfortunate relatives who implored him to obtain whatever information he could. "In the end," he says, "every index card was to me a heart-rending personal appeal."[52] This experience confirmed his dislike of a purely abstract system of thought and his preference for philosophizing concretely *hic et nunc.* He was to say: "I am inclined to deny that any work is philosophical if we cannot discern in it what may be called the sting of reality."[53]

In our own country that "sting of reality"
was felt by William James. For many years he
had poor health, which included backaches, eye
trouble, indigestion, insomnia. He suffered
from severe spells of depression which became
worse between the ages of twenty and thirty.
He had many philosophical doubts that he
could not resolve, and he had a feeling of the
purposelessness of his existence.[54] His mother
once said of him in a letter: "His temperament
is a morbidly hopeless one, and with this he has
to contend all the time, as well as with his physical disability."[55] But when he was twenty-
eight, he experienced what he called in his journal a crisis in his life. This was the reading
of some essays of Charles Renouvier which
stressed free will. He then and there resolved
that his first act of free will would be to believe
in free will.[56] He later told his father that the
reading of Renouvier was one of the things that
cleared up his mind and restored it to sanity.[57]
Applying his new insight, he said in "Is Life
Worth Living?" that if we believe that life *is*
worth living, our belief will help create the fact,
and in "The Will to Believe," that, under certain conditions, faith in a fact can help create
the fact.[58] He shared with others a thesis that
had worked well for him in his personal life.

More recently, Father Norris Clarke of Fordham University told of a boyhood experience that may have started him on his career as a metaphysician. At the age of fourteen or fifteen he liked to climb up the sheer five-hundred-foot high cliffs of the New Jersey Palisades, just above the sign that said "No Climbing Here." The first time he tried it he got stuck two-thirds of the way up and could move neither up nor down. Looking down, he saw traffic stopped on the river road, motorists shouting at him and policemen yelling they were going to arrest him. As he studied his situation more carefully, he noticed that there was a bulge of rock to his right with a niche for his foot beyond it, but he could not see if there was a niche for his hand higher up. Not knowing whether life or death awaited him, he decided to swing around the rock into space. Luckily there was a handhold. He climbed up the rest of the cliff and fled into the bushes. Commenting on the philosophical significance of this experience, he says:

> . . . something momentous happened to me as I swung out into space, suspended between being and non-being. At that moment I suddenly broke through to the felt awareness of existence as such; I felt the bittersweet but extraordinarily exhilarating taste of actual existence in my mouth, the taste of its infinite preciousness and yet precariousness and of its unspeakable difference from non-existence.[59]

He adds that though this happened fifty years ago, it still nourishes his metaphysical intuition.

Sometimes a person wonders and philosophizes in response to a challenge posed by other thinkers. To list just a few examples: Plato's answer, in the *Republic,* to the Sophists' view of law and justice;[60] Aristotle's analysis of motion in the *Physics,* in response to the Eleatic denial of change;[61] Averroes' retort to Algazel in the *Destructio Destructionum Philosophiae Algazelis;*[64] Kant's acknowledgement in the *Prolegomena* that the suggestion of David Hume was the very thing which first interrupted his dogmatic slumber and gave his investigations in the field of speculative philosophy a new direction;[63] Jacques Maritain's rejection of the materialism of his Sorbonne teachers and his recovery of a sense of the absolute after hearing the lectures of Bergson.[64]

In a number of briefly stated miscellaneous examples we have indicated how a person's philosophical thinking has proceeded from some personal or intellectual experience. Let us look — more fully this time — at one more example, that of St. Thomas Aquinas whose memory we honor today. He, too, had experiences that aroused his wonder and invited him to philosophize.

In 1231 at the age of five or six Thomas Aquinas was sent to the abbey of Montecassino. In this Benedictine environment he received his basic education and his early religious training. It was here, so far as we know, that his wonder began. An early biographer records that "earnestly and often" Thomas would ask his Benedictine teachers: "What is God?"[65] His efforts to answer that question were to lead to the hundreds of pages on God in the *Summa Theologiae.*

On the advice of the abbot of Montecassino, when Thomas was about fourteen, he went to the University of Naples to study the liberal arts. Here he was introduced to Aristotle's metaphysics and natural philosophy. At Naples he also became acquainted with some Dominican friars and made his decision to join their new order which emphasized study as a means to its apostolate of preaching.[66] His vocation as a Dominican was to influence all of his further activity.

From 1248 to 1252 Thomas studied at Cologne under Albert, a man of extraordinary learning who knew the works recently translated from Greek and Arabic as well as the writings of Christian authors.[67] Like Albert, Thomas would always have an open-minded

interest in the writings of both Christian and
non-Christian thinkers. He was to encounter
both traditions at Paris, the first represented
mainly by the thought of St. Augustine; the
second, mainly by the works of Aristotle and
his Arabian commentators.

A conflict of the non-Christian with the
Christian tradition raised questions that caused
Thomas to wonder. A brief account of the
background of the conflict will help us see the
problem to which Thomas responded.

During the twelfth and thirteenth centuries
the works of Aristotle, accompanied by commentaries by Arabian thinkers, came into
Europe in Latin translation. Although Aristotle
had previously been known and admired as
"The Philosopher" for his logical works, Christians now had access to his *Physics, Metaphysics,*
and *De Anima,* and to the commentaries of
Averroes. But this "new" Aristotle seemed at
times to be denying what Christian teaching
affirmed, for example, personal immortality
and creation. And since Christians had identi-
fied The Philosopher with philosophy, it seemed
to them that philosophy itself was in contradiction to some truths of faith. This raised the
question: How is it possible to be both a good
philosopher and a good Christian? Some who

chose to be good Christians stressed faith at the expense of reason and philosophy. Some who chose to be philosophers stressed reason at the expense of faith. The Latin Averroists whom Thomas knew during his years at Paris tried to work out a compromise.

Some Averroists held that through philosophy they reached necessary conclusions of reason, but that these conclusions should not be asserted as true if they were in contradiction to faith. Though this position, strictly speaking, was not a theory of double truth, it seemed to imply that the best effort of reason cannot reach truth or that faith is concerned with something that reason could find false and impossible.[68] It still looked as though we had to choose between an allegiance to faith (and hence to God) or to reason (and hence to our humanity).

This was the context that raised some of the principal problems that Thomas wondered about. What *is* the relation of faith and reason? Must we reject reason to be good Christians? Must we reject faith to be good philosophers?

Though we cannot here follow each step in his quest for some answers, we can briefly note that Thomas was challenged to work out the distinction and mutual relations of reason and faith. He was to conclude that reason and faith are two different motives for assenting to something as true. When we accept something as true by faith, we do so because God has said it; to know something by reason is to accept it as true because we see it by the natural light of our own mind.[69] Some truths are both attainable by reason and revealed by God. Others, those that exceed the power of our reason, are knowable only by revelation.[70]

In Thomas' view, reason and faith can help each other. Reason can make some truths of faith clearer to our understanding, and faith helps reason because it goes beyond it and perfects it. Thomas says that "the truth that the human reason is naturally endowed to know cannot be opposed to the truth of the Christian faith."[71] Truth cannot contradict truth.

But it is one thing to speak in general of the amicable relation of reason and faith and another to apply this to specific cases of seeming conflict.

Aristotle, as interpreted by Averroes, seemed to be saying that only one agent and one possible intellect exist for all men and that the world is necessary and eternal. This implicit denial of personal immortality and creation contradicted the teachings of Christian faith. Christian thinkers wondered how to resolve these particular instances of a conflict between philosophical reason and Christian faith. In response to this wonder Thomas was to show that reason, when rightly used, does not end up with conclusions that contradict faith.

If it were true that there is one intellect for the whole human race and if we do not have our own individual intellects, this would leave us without any incorruptible part of the soul, and so without a philosophical basis for affirming a natural personal immortality. But Thomas shows that sound philosophy requires us to reject the view that there is just one intellect for the whole human race. The evident fact is that "this individual man knows" and the only way we can properly account for that fact is to acknowledge that each one of us has his own intellect. [72]

On the question of the eternity of the world, Thomas holds that if God freely willed the world to exist, we cannot prove either that it had to exist always or that it had to have a beginning in time. Though we can know from faith that the world did have a beginning in time, either alternative is philosophically possible. But whatever the world's duration, it is a created world that owes its existence to God. [73]

Though reason alone does not know all that is knowable, yet, when it is rightly used, it does not contradict faith. Because of the Latin Averroists, Thomas wondered and wrote about problems that he otherwise might not have confronted.

The very titles of such works as *De unitate intellectus contra Averroistas* and *De aeternitate mundi contra murmurantes* name problems that challenged him to think. There were other challenges as well, for example, those reflected in the *Contra impugnantes Dei cultum et religionem,* a refutation of William of Saint-Amour's attack on the mendicant teachers at Paris, and the *Summa contra Gentiles,* a manual written at the request of Raymond of Penafort, for the use of Dominican missionaries working among Moslems, Jews, and pagans in Spain.[74]

Sometimes what Thomas wondered about resulted from the requirements of his work as a teacher or from his attempt as a Christian to answer requests for help when he could. His commentaries on the Bible, on Dionysius (whom we speak of today as Pseudo-Dionysius), on Boethius, on Peter Lombard, on Aristotle, grew out of his teaching.[75] The five hundred and ten articles of the *Disputed Questions* and the twelve *Quodlibetal Questions* are the fruit of those lively academic exercises at Paris that closely reflected what both students and masters were wondering about.[76] The *Summa Theologiae* was written to instruct beginners in sacred doctrine in a way that follows the order of the subject matter.[77] Within his broad plan of talking about God Himself and then about the things coming forth from God as their beginning and returning to God as their end, he gives a philosophical treatment of many of the topics of the two thousand six hundred and forty-four articles that are presented within the *Summa's* five hundred and twelve questions.[78] Looking just at the statistics, one might venture to say that scarcely any thinker has wondered about more questions than Thomas Aquinas.

Though his duties as a teacher gave him more than enough questions to wonder about, he also sometimes received letters asking for help. A Friar Baxianus from the Dominican convent in Venice wanted answers to thirty-six questions within four days. Thomas responded with, literally, the patience of a saint:

> Although I have been very busy, I have put aside for a time the things that I should do and have decided to answer individually the questions which you proposed . . . .[79]

A few weeks later, during a Holy Week Mass,

Thomas received a special letter from the Master General, John of Vercelli, who wanted an immediate reply to forty-two questions. Fortunately thirty-six of them were very similar to those he had recently answered for the friar from Venice, but Thomas immediately suspended his participation in Holy Week services and worked steadily at the answers to the forty-two questions until he completed them on the following day, which was Holy Thursday.[80]

Just looking at the list of St. Thomas' works makes us realize that they came out of an intensely busy life of teaching, of taking and supporting a stand on controversial topics, and of responding to requests for help from Popes, fellow friars, other masters, and students.[81]

It is clear that as a thinker Thomas developed by wondering about and working on problem after problem, arising from, though not limited to his own thirteenth century life-experience as a teacher, scholar, and monk.

In the philosophers whom we have considered we have seen how personal and intellectual experiences in their lives aroused their wonder and stimulated reflection. Let us now look at the philosophical basis for this connection between life and philosophy. Such a basis can be found in St. Thomas' view of the nature of man.

III. Philosophical Basis for How Philosophy Begins

This being who wonders, who asks questions, who tries to escape ignorance and reach understanding participates in spirit, yet also is matter. Aided by Aristotle, Thomas saw a matter/form composition in man, though the explanation of the unique way in which form is related to matter in us was his own contribution.

In Aristotle's context a corporeal being is composed of two principles, prime matter and substantial form, matter being the wholly potential, determinable principle and form the determining, specifying, actuating principle. In a living being the substantial form is the soul, the principle of life and source of a living being's activities. It is related to the body as an actuality to that of which it is the actuality.[82]

Thomas, seeing man as one being, though composite in nature, also thinks that the soul is the substantial form of the matter of the body.[83] He shows that all of man's activities, including his knowing and loving, are affected by this hylemorphic composition. But since he sees, too, that the soul has an act in which the body does not share essentially (for example, understanding), he would add that the soul is subsistent.[84] His view that the human soul is both subsistent and a form of matter was a puzzling paradox to other Aristotelian thinkers, but it expressed for Thomas the uniqueness of man.[85] The older view had been that every form of matter was a determining, specifying principle that operates and exists only through matter. Thomas, however, distinguished two kinds of forms of matter: (1) a material form that is immersed in matter and exists only through the being of the composite; and (2) a form that is not immersed in matter, but exists through its own being, and through its being the composite exists. It is this second meaning that describes how the human soul is the form of the body. The soul gives being, in the manner of a formal cause, to the whole composite so that by one *esse,* that of the soul, the whole composite exists.[86] "Existentially considered," as one commentator has said, "it is the body that is in the soul, not the soul that is in the body."[87]

But if the soul is the kind of form that gives being to the composite, then it is a substance, and that raises the question: Why should this immaterial substance be joined to a body? Thomas answers that it is substance insofar as it is subsistent, but it is not a complete substance; it does not have all that it needs to

perfect itself. It is the lowest of intellectual substances (in contrast with angels) and therefore
needs to be joined to a body to achieve its perfection as spirit.[88]

There are two ways we can look at ourselves
in the hierarchy of being, and both help in our
self-understanding. The more usual way is to
see ourselves as highest among living corporeal
beings. In addition to having the powers of
growth, nutrition, and reproduction which are
found among plants, and in addition to having
the power of sensation found in animals, we
have the power of thought. By the greater im-
manence and range of our activities, we surpass
plants and animals. But Thomas also invited us
to look at ourselves from a different perspective
—as not only above brute animals but also as
lower than angels. This, too, can help us understand ourselves and our knowing.

For Thomas the highest created perfection
is found in angels or spiritual substances. "They
are related to lower creatures as the perfect is to
the imperfect," he says.[89] At the highest point
in our nature we touch the lowest point of the
nature of angels and thus share, though in a
weakened way, in their full intellectual light.[90]

Angels' intellects are receptive only of what
is above them. Together with their own natures,

angels received from God a knowledge of things
both in their universal nature and in their singu-
larity. They have no need of composing and
dividing and reasoning. As immaterial intellectual beings they know intelligibles directly.[91]

As compared with the full light of intellect in
angels, our reason arises in the shadow of intel-
ligence *(in umbra intelligentiae).* [92] Because we are
by nature embodied or incarnate spirits, we start
from our location in matter. Our way of getting
at essences of things is by abstracting from material things. For the perfection of our knowing we
need to judge and to reason. Our knowing
resembles angelic knowing in the awareness of
first principles with which reasoning begins (the
habit of *intellectus*) and in the terminating point
of our reasoning (the understanding expressed
in the conclusion), but the process by which we
move from premises to conclusion results from
our involvement in matter, motion, and time.[93]

Thomas says that we know discursively,
through continuity and time. Unlike angels we do
not possess the perfection of knowing connaturally
from the beginning of our existence. Rather we, in
our knowing, move from being able to understand
to actually understanding. Thus time, the
measure of motion, touches our knowing — and
not just once, but again and again.[94]

We do not possess either the whole of our life or the whole of our knowing simultaneously, for we live our life successively. At each stage, whatever we encounter in matter and time can serve as a new *terminus a quo* from which we can move, in our knowing, to a new *terminus ad quem.* Compared with angels, we must take, as Thomas says, "the longer way" to complete our intellectual nature.[95] But in this work, both Thomas and Aristotle agree, "time is our good partner."[96]

Perhaps we wish that like angels we could grasp truth directly. We might like our words to be welcomed as angelic salutations, but since we are human beings, our loftiest flights of thought take off from earthly and temporal experiences like, for example, the stealing of some pears, being imprisoned in a dungeon, or climbing the Jersey Palisades. We are not extra-terrestrial beings, accidentally left behind on this earth. This is where we were born, and this is where we develop our thought.

Herein lies the significance of biography for our philosophical knowing. Each temporal and earthly experience can actuate our potentiality for knowing. Each is an invitation to think. Through successive acts of thinking about successive experiences our philosophical life develops and our intellect *moves* towards achieving its fulfillment.

As Anton Pegis has said:

> . . . for St. Thomas the substance of man's temporal
> duration is nothing less than his becoming as spirit,
> his growth and coming of age as a spiritual being.
> . . . seen in this way, the existence of man in history,
> that very existence of which biographies are written,
> is a record not merely of what man has done, but of
> the growth and building of what he *is* . . . .[97]

But lest there be any misunderstanding,
one thing should be noted explicitly: Though
we are incarnate beings whose perfection as
spirit depends on our use of the world of matter
and time, this does not mean that our knowing
is *limited* to individual, concrete temporal instances that we directly encounter. St. Thomas
often reminds us that from material singulars
or particulars we abstract universals.[98] While
informing matter, the human soul has acts going beyond matter.[99] And while subject to
time, the human mind in itself is above that
time which is the measure of motion.[100] Our
mind like a small spark from a fire *(scintilla . . .
ex igne evolans)* shares in intellectual nature.[101]

At once highest of corporeal beings and
lowest of intellectual beings, we are at the
boundary line of the world of matter and the
world of spirit and both of these worlds meet
within us. Neither animal nor angel, we are at
once immanent in the body and yet transcen-

dent, subject to time and yet surpassing it.[102] As St. Thomas says, it is as though we exist on the horizon of time and eternity.[103]

Reflecting on our unique position in the hierarchy of being helps us to understand both our nature and our knowing. In particular, it helps us to see how the successive encounters of an incarnate spirit developing in the world of matter and time can arouse a wonder that leads to a philosophical knowing.

IV. Epilogue

Having considered how philosophy begins, we might appropriately add a few words on how philosophy ends.

As a human enterprise, philosophy will continue so long as there is some human being who wonders. But how does it end for the individual?

Our wonder leads to inquiry because we desire to know. The good of our intellect is the knowledge of truth, but sometimes we do not succeed in reaching that end.[104] Philosophy can end in frustration.

Sometimes we lose touch with the reality that aroused our wonder; we spin webs of abstractions that obscure rather than reveal the

hidden cause we are seeking. Sometimes we are
needlessly disputatious because, as a result of
the limitations of our experience and of our
mode of knowing, we may mistake a part for
the whole reality we are trying to understand.
You may recall the old story of the blind men
and the elephant. The man who placed his
hand against the elephant's broad and sturdy
side said, "The elephant is very like a wall." The
second blind man, feeling of the round,
smooth, sharp tusk, said, "This wonder of an
elephant is very like a spear." The third, hap-
pening to take the squirming trunk within his
hands, thought the elephant was like a snake.
The fourth, feeling the animal's leg, thought the
elephant was like a tree; the fifth, touching the
ear, compared the elephant to a fan. The sixth,
seizing the tail, said the elephant was like a
rope. These men, as the poet remarks:

> Disputed loud and long
> Each in his opinion
> Exceeding stiff and strong,
> Though each was partly in the right
> And all were in the wrong! [105]

We do not always know whether we have
taken into account all the aspects that are essen-
tial to explaining something. And sometimes,
even when we are aware of them, our fascination

with one aspect results in a neglect of the other relevant factors. It is not easy to achieve a complete and balanced view. Truth, as Plato held, is akin to good proportion. We do not always have that most desirable quality of a philosopher: "a naturally well-proportioned and gracious mind, which will move spontaneously towards the true being of everything."[106]

But, if we wish to achieve the end of philosophy, we can compensate for the limits of our individual vision, by learning from our predecessors. We can look at what they point out to us. St. Thomas advises us to love both those whose opinion we follow and those whose opinion we reject, for "both," he says, "diligently sought for truth and helped us, in so doing."[107] He himself, as we know, learned from a variety of thinkers, including such ancient philosophers as Plato and Aristotle, the Christian St. Augustine, the Moslem Avicenna and Averroes, and the Jewish rabbi, Moses Maimonides. It was St. Thomas' conviction that "every truth, whoever speaks it, is from the Holy Spirit."[108]

Though we are finite and fallible beings, we may, with the aid of others and the effort of our own minds, come to see things in an intelligible context. The philosophy that begins in wonder about lived experience and proceeds to reflection can end by at least partially fulfilling one of the deepest needs that we have: the need to understand.

St. Thomas thinks that our search for truth should eventually lead us to God, since the inquiry that begins with wonder cannot come to rest until we know the first cause who is God. The ultimate end of our quest will consist in seeing God in his essence.[109] This end is not attainable now, but according to St. Thomas, even the pursuit of wisdom especially joins us to God in friendship.[110] Philosophy is neither the whole of a human life nor is it our total felicity, but it is a beginning of our beatitude.[111] The contemplation of truth that will reach its fulfillment in the life to come, begins in this life with our wonder.

Having seen how philosophy begins and having noted how it can end, we might well heed this advice of an ancient Greek thinker:

Let no one when young delay to study philosophy, nor when he is old grow weary of his study. For no one can come too early or too late to secure the health of his soul. And the man who says that the age for philosophy has either not yet come or has gone by is like the man who says that the age for happiness has not yet come or has passed away. Wherefore both when young and when old a person should study philosophy . . . .[112]

NOTES

1. Al-Ghazali, *Tahafut Al-Falasifah,* tr. by S. A. Kamali (Lahore: Pakistan Philosophical Congress, 1958), p. 4.

2. Diogenes Laertius, *Lives of Eminent Philosophers,* tr. by R. D. Hicks (London: William Heinemann, & New York: G. P. Putnam, 1925), vol. I, p. 35; Plato, *Theaetetus* 174, tr. by B. Jowett, in *The Dialogues of Plato* (New York: Random House, 1937), vol. II, p. 176.

3. *Louisa May Alcott: Her Life, Letters, and Journals,* ed. by E. D. Cheney (Boston: Roberts Brothers, 1890), p. 315.

4. *The Complete Plays of Gilbert and Sullivan* (New York: Modern Library, n.d.), p. 307.

5. Aristotle, *Metaphysics* I, 1, 980a and 2, 982b, tr. by W. D. Ross in R. McKeon, *The Basic Works of Aristotle* (New York: Random House, 1941), p. 689 & p. 692.

6. Plato, *Theaetetus* 155, in *ed. cit.,* p. 157.

7. Thomas Aquinas, *Summa Theologiae* I, q. 114, a. 4; III, q. 15, a. 8 (Ottawa: Institute of Medieval Studies, 1941); *Summa contra Gentiles* III, c. 101 (Rome: Vatican Library, Leonine ed., 1934); *In II Sent.,* dist. 18, q. 1, a. 3, sol. in *Scriptum super Libros Sententiarum,* ed. R. P. Mandonnet (Paris: Lethielleux, 1929).

8. René Descartes, in *Les Passions de l'Âme,* ed. G. Rodis-Lewis (Paris: J. Vrin, 1955), part 2, art. 70, p. 116, says: "L'admiration est une subite surprise de l'âme, qui fait qu'elle se porte à considerer avec attention les objets qui semblent rares et extraordinaires." And Arthur Schopenhauer after noting that". . . very early, with the first dawn of reflection, that wonder already appears, which is some day to become the mother of metaphysics," thinks it is the knowledge of death and the consideration of the suffering and misery in life which gives the strongest impulse to philosophical reflection. He adds: "If our life were endless and painless, it would perhaps occur to no one to ask why the world exists and is just the kind of world it is; but everything would be taken just as a matter of course." See *The World as Will and as Idea,* tr. by R. B. Haldane

& John Kemp (London: Kegan Paul, Trench, Trubner, 1896), vol. II, Bk. I, ch. 17, pp. 359-360; vol. III, Bk. IV, ch. 41, p. 249.

9. John Dewey, *How We Think* (Boston, New York, Chicago: D. C. Heath, 1910), pp. 10-11.

10. William James, *Pragmatism,* Lecture II (New York: Meridian Books, 1959), pp. 50-51.

11. Jessie Corrigan Pegis, "The Eyes of Wonder," in *America,* vol. 61 (July 1, 1939), p. 284. Reprinted with permission of the author and with permission of America Press, Inc., 106 West 56th Street, New York, N.Y. 10019, © 1939, All rights reserved.

12. Alfred Lord Tennyson, "Flower in the Crannied Wall," in Robert Shafer, ed., *From Beowulf to Thomas Hardy* (Garden City, N.Y.: Doubleday, Doran & Co., 1931), vol. II, p. 491.

13. *The Confessions of St. Augustine* IX, #23-25 (New York: Airmont Publishing Co., 1969), pp. 162-164.

14. William James, "The Sentiment of Rationality," in *The Will to Believe and Other Essays in Popular Philosophy* (Dover Publications, 1956), p. 74.

15. Samuel Johnson, *The Rambler,* No. 137 (Tuesday 9 July, 1751) in R. Shafer, *op. cit.,* vol. I, p. 636.

16. The distinction between "wondering-why" and "wondering-at" is made by E. Mascall in "The Death of Wonder," *The Way,* vol. II (January, 1971), p. 35.

17. Thomas Aquinas, *In Met.* I, lect. 3, #55, in *In Duodecim Libros Metaphysicorum Aristotelis Expositio* (Turin & Rome: Marietti, 1950).

18. *Ibid.,* #53; Aristotle, *Met.* I, 2, 982b.

19. Thomas Aquinas, *In Met.* I, lect. 3, #55 & #67.

20. Thomas Aquinas, *In II Sent.,* dist. 18, q. 1, a. 3, sol.; *Quaestiones Disputatae de Potentia Dei,* q. 6, a. 6, in *Quaestiones Disputatae* (Turin & Rome: Marietti, 1949), vol. II; *Sum. Theol.* I, q. 105, a. 8; I-II, q. 32, a. 8.

21. *Sum. Theol.* I-II, q. 42, a. 1, resp. & ad 4; II-II, q. 180, a. 3, ad 3; *Quaestiones Disputatae de Veritate,* q. 26, a. 4, ad 7, in *Quaestiones Disputatae* (Turin & Rome: Marietti, 1949), vol. I.

22. *Sum. Theol.* I, q. 81, a. 2; I-II, q. 23, a. 1; I-II, q. 41, a. 2, resp. & ad 3; I-II, q. 42, a. 3; *In III Sent.,* dist. 26, q. 1, a. 3, sol.

23. *Sum. Theol.* I-II, q. 42, a. 4.

24. *Ibid.,* I-II, q. 76, a. 2.

25. *Ibid.,* I, q. 12, a. 1; I-II, q. 3, a. 8; I-II, q. 32, a. 8; *Cont. Gent.,* III c. 25.

26. *Sum. Theol.* I, q. 81, a. 2; I-II. q. 23, a. 1; I-II, q. 41, a. 2, ad 3.

27. In *Sum. Theol.* I-II, q. 42, a. 1, St. Thomas quotes this approvingly from St. Augustine.

28. *Ibid.,* I-II, q. 32, a. 8.

29. *Ibid.,* I, q. 14, a. 1, & q. 80, a. 1.

30. Attributed to Cosmo Monkhouse in Burton E. Stevenson, ed., *The Home Book of Verse for Young Folks* (New York: Holt, Rinehart & Winston, 1929), p. 195.

31. *Sum. Theol.* I, q. 84, a. 1 & a. 2.

32. Walt Whitman, *Leaves of Grass,* ed. H. W. Blodgett & S. Bradley (New York: New York University Press, 1965), p. 364. I am indebted to James E. Royce, S.J., *Man and Meaning* (New York: McGraw-Hill, 1969), p. 119, for suggesting this example.

33. *Sum. Theol.* I, q. 16, a. 1 & 2; I, q. 85, articles 1, 2, 5, 6; *De Veritate* q. 1, a. 3 & a. 9; *In Met.* VI, lect. 4, #1232-1233.

34. *Sum. Theol.* I, q. 79, a. 8; I, q. 85, a. 5; *In Met,* I, lect. 3, #67.

35. Etienne Gilson, *The Unity of Philosophical Experience* (New York: Charles Scribner's Sons, 1937), pp. 300-301.

36. Anton C. Pegis, "Who Reads Aquinas?" in *Thought,* vol. 13 (1967), p. 496.

37. Michel de Montaigne, "Of the Education of Children," in *Montaigne: Selected Essays* (Ann Arbor, Mich.: Edwards Brothers. Inc., 1946), p. 158 & p. 160.

38. James Boswell, *The Life of Samuel Johnson* (London: J. M. Dent & Co., 1901), vol. 2, p. 344.

39. Cf. *Phaedo* in *The Dialogues of Plato,* tr. B. Jowett, vol. 1, pp. 441-501.

40. The modern "serenity prayer" is as follows: "God grant me the serenity to accept the things I cannot change, the courage to change the things I can, and the wisdom to know the difference." Cf. Epictetus, *Encheiridion,* Sec. #1-2, 5, in *Epictetus, The Discourses as reported by Arrian, The Manual and Fragments,* tr. by W. A. Oldfather (Cambridge: Harvard University Press & London: W. Heinemann, 1952), vol. 2, pp. 485, 487, 489.

41. Boethius, *The Consolation of Philosophy,* tr. by W. V. Cooper (New York: Modern Library, 1943).

42. *The Story of Abelard's Adversities: A Translation of the Historia Calamitatum* by J. T. Muckle (Toronto: Pontifical Institute of Mediaeval Studies, 1964), pp. 12-23, 43-52.

43. *Ibid.,* pp. 26-40.

44. *Ibid.,* pp. 25, 39, 79.

45. St. Augustine, *Confessions,* II, #4-10 in *ed. cit.,* pp. 26-30. On evil, see also Books III, IV, V, & esp. VII; *De Libero Arbitrio* II & III in J. P. Migne, *Patrologia Latina,* vol. 32, 1221-1310; *De Genesi contra Manichaeos, PL,* vol. 34, 173-220.

46. René Descartes, *Discourse on Method,* I, tr. by Donald Cress (Indianapolis: Hackett Publishing Co., 1980), pp. 4-5.

47. *Ibid.* & Parts II, III, IV. —Gilson points out in *The Unity of Philosophical Experience,* pp. 130-134, that the professor who taught Descartes mathematics at La Flèche was a Father François, S.J., a man who was interested in applied mathematics, but in Jesuit schools of the time the authority in the field was Father Clavius who stresses in the introduction to the 1611 edition of his *Mathematical Works* the certainty and demonstrative character of mathematical disciplines.

48. Søren Kierkegaard, *Either/Or,* vol. I, tr. by D. F. Swenson & L. M. Swenson, vol. II, tr. by Walter Lowrie (Princeton: Princeton University Press, 1944); *Stages on Life's Way,* tr. by Walter Lowrie (Princeton: Princeton University Press, 1940); *Concluding Unscientific Postscript,* tr. by D. F. Swenson (Princeton: Princeton University Press, 1941).

49. On Kierkegaard's personal experience of the three stages, see *Søren Kierkegaard's Journals and Papers,* tr. by H. V. Hong and E. H. Hong (Bloomington, Ind.: Indiana University Press, 1978), vol. 5, p. 36 (#5100): "I have vainly sought an anchor in the boundless sea of pleasure . . . . I have felt the counterfeit enthusiasm it is capable of producing. I have also felt the boredom . . . which follows on its heels." See also p. 35 (#5100), p. 101 (#5231), p. 111 (#5280), p. 234 (#5664). —On p. 197 (Feb. 6, 1842), he said: "The esthetic is above all my element. As soon as the ethical asserts itself, it easily gains too much power over me." And on p. 377 (#6001): "I could have made my life easier, humanly speaking . . . . But do I have the right to do this to God?" See also p. 361 (#5962), and for references to Abraham, see p. 163 (#5485) and pp. 224-225 (#5646).

   For interpretive comment, see William Barrett, *Irrational Man* (Garden City, N.Y.: Doubleday Anchor Books, 1962), pp. 153-155; James Collins, *The Mind of Kierkegaard* (London: Secker & Warburg, 1954), pp. 8-11.

50. Frederick Copleston, S.J., *Contemporary Philosophy* (Westminster, Md.: Newman Press, 1956), p. 128.

51. Gabriel Marcel, *Creative Fidelity,* tr. by Robert Rosthal (New York: Noonday Press, 1964), p. 64.

52. Gabriel Marcel, "An Essay in Autobiography," in *The Philosophy of Existentialism,* tr. by Manya Harari (Secaucus, N.J.: Citadel Press, 1973), p. 121. See also *Gabriel Marcel, interrogé par Pierre Boutang,* ed. J.-M. Place (Paris: Jouve, 1977), pp. 15-17.

53. Marcel, *Creative Fidelity,* p. 64.

54. See Henry James' comments in *The Letters of William James,* edited by his son Henry James (Boston: Atlantic Monthly Press, 1920), vol. I, pp. 84-85, 140-147; and Ralph B. Perry, *The Thought and Character of William James* (Boston: Little, Brown & Co., 1935), vol. I, pp. 220, 233-234, 320-324, 328.

55. Quoted from an unpublished letter of Mrs. Henry James, Sr., to Henry James, Jr., in F. O. Mattheissen, *The James Family* (New York: Alfred A. Knopf, 1947), p. 221.

56. *Letters of William James,* ed. by his son, vol. I, p. 147.

57. *Ibid.,* p. 169. See letter of Henry James, Sr., to Henry James, Jr., dated Mar. 18, 1873.

58. William James, "Is Life Worth Living?" and "The Will to Believe," in *The Will to Believe and Other Essays in Popular Philosophy,* p. 62 & p. 25.

59. W. Norris Clarke, S.J., "Medalist's Address: The Philosophical Importance of Doing One's Autobiography," in *Proceedings of the American Catholic Philosophical Association* (Washington, D.C.: Catholic University of America, 1980), vol. LIV, pp. 20-21. Quoted with the permission of the author.

60. On the Sophists' position, see Antiphon the Sophist in Kathleen Freeman, *Ancilla to the Pre-Socratic Philosophers* (Oxford: Basil Blackwell, 1948), p. 147. For Plato's statement of the question and answer, see especially *Republic* II, IV, IX, and the speech of Callicles in the *Gorgias,* 483-484A in B. Jowett's translation, *The Dialogues of Plato,* vol. I, pp. 543-544.

61. Aristotle, *Physics* I & II, in McKeon, *Basic Works of Aristotle.*

62. Averroes, *Destructio Destructionum Philosophiae Algazelis,* in the Latin version of Calo Calonymos, ed. by Beatrice H. Zedler (Milwaukee: Marquette University Press, 1961).

63. Immanuel Kant, *Prolegomena to Any Future Metaphysics,* ed. Paul Carus (Chicago: Open Court, 1933), p. 7.

64. Jacques Maritain, in *I Believe: The Personal Philosophies of Twenty-three Eminent Men and Women of our Time* (London: Geo. Allen & Unwin, 1940, reprinted 1962), p. 225.

65. Peter Calo, *Vita,* c. 3, from *Fontes Vitae Sancti Thomae Aquinatis,* in Kenelm Foster, O.P., *The Life of Saint Thomas Aquinas: Biographical Documents* (London: Longmans, Green; Baltimore: Helicon Press, 1959), p. 15. — See also Vernon J. Bourke, *Aquinas' Search for Wisdom* (Milwaukee: Bruce, 1964), pp. 7-17; Angelus Walz, O.P., *Saint Thomas Aquinas: A Biographical Study* (Westminster, Md.: Newman, 1951), pp. 8-18; James A. Weisheipl, O.P., *Friar Thomas d'Aquino* (Garden City, N.Y.: Doubleday & Co., 1974), pp. 10-12.

66. Bernard Gui, *Life of St. Thomas Aquinas,* in Foster, *op. cit.,* p. 27; Bourke, *op. cit.,* pp. 19-29, 33-36; Walz, *op. cit.,* 17-31; Weisheipl, *op. cit.,* pp. 12-18.

67. Bourke, *op. cit.,* pp. 40-51; Walz, *op. cit.,* pp. 43-53; Weisheipl, *op. cit.,* pp. 36-45.

68. Thomas Aquinas, *De Unitate Intellectus contra Averroistas,* c. 5, #123; see *On the Unity of the Intellect against the Averroists,* tr. by Beatrice H. Zedler (Milwaukee: Marquette University Press, 1968), p. 74. — For the context of the problem see B. H. Zedler, "Theory of Double Truth," in *New Catholic Encyclopedia* (New York: McGraw-Hill, 1967), vol. 4, 1022-1023.

69. Thomas Aquinas, *Sum. Theol.* II-II, q. 1, a. 1, a. 4, a. 5; *De Ver.,* q. 14, a. 8.

70. Thomas Aquinas, *Cont. Gent.* I, c. 3, c. 4; *Sum. Theol.,* I, q. 1, a. 1.

71. *Cont. Gent.* I, c. 7. See also *Sum. Theol.* I, q. 1, a. 5, ad 2; *De Ver.,* q. 14, a. 10, ad 9.

72. For a more detailed account of Averroes' position, see B. H. Zedler, "Averroes on the Possible Intellect," in *Proceedings of the American Catholic Philosophical Association,* vol. XXV (1951), pp. 164-178. — For St. Thomas' answer to the challenge of the Latin Averroists, see *De Unitate Intellectus, tr. cit.,* Foreward, #2, p. 22, & Chapters 3, 4, 5.

73. *Sum. Theol.* I, q. 46, a. 1 & a. 2; *Cont Gent.* II, c. 32-38.
    As Armand Maurer says in *Medieval Philosophy* (New
    York: Random House, 1962), p. 174: "St. Thomas dis-
    tinguishes the problem of the temporal origin of the uni-
    verse from that of its origin in being. He considers its
    ontological origin or creation, rationally demonstrable,
    but not its origin in time. The eternity or non-eternity of
    the universe must remain an open question to the philo-
    sopher; only by faith do we know that it had a beginning
    in time." For further texts on the problem, see *St. Thomas
    Aquinas, Siger of Brabant, St. Bonaventure on The Eternity of
    the World,* tr. by Cyril Vollert, S.J., Lottie H. Kendzier-
    ski, Paul M. Byrne (Milwaukee: Marquette University
    Press, 1964).

74. The *Contra impugnantes Dei cultum et religionem* was written
    in 1256 against William of Saint Amour's *De periculis
    novissimorum temporum.* Between 1269 and 1272, in
    response to further attacks by a follower of William,
    Gerard of Abbeville, Thomas wrote *De perfectione vitae
    spiritualis* and *Contra pestiferam doctrinam retrahentium pueros
    a religionis ingressu.* See Weisheipl, *op. cit.,* pp. 383-384.

    On the *Summa contra Gentiles,* see St. Thomas, *Cont.
    Gent.* I, c. 2; A. C. Pegis, General Introduction to his
    translation of Book I of *Summa contra Gentiles: On the Truth
    of the Catholic Faith* (Garden City, N.Y.: Image Books,
    1955), pp. 20-21; M. D. Chenu, *Toward Understanding
    Saint Thomas,* tr. by A. M. Landry & D. Hughes
    (Chicago: Regnery, 1964), pp. 288-292; Weisheipl, *op.
    cit.,* pp. 129-134, 359-360.

75. Chenu, *op. cit.,* Chapters VI, VII, VIII.

76. On the nature and background of the disputed questions
    and the quodlibetal questions, see *Ibid.,* Chapter II &
    IX; Bourke, *op. cit.,* pp. 94-98; Weisheipl, *op. cit.,* pp.
    123-127; P. Mandonnet, Introduction to *Quaestiones dis-
    putatae* (Paris: Lethielleux, 1925), vol. I, pp. 1-9.

    One of the disputed questions, *De Potentia Dei,* has
    been interpreted as the complete Christian answer that
    Thomas Aquinas gave to the emanationism of Avicenna,

another interest of his time. See Father Maurice Bouyges, S.J., "L'idée génératrice du *De Potentia* de saint Thomas," *Revue de philosophie* II (1931), pp. 113-131, 246-268, and B.H. Zedler, "St. Thomas and Avicenna in the *De Potentia Dei,"* *Traditio,* vol. VI (1948), pp. 105-159, and "The Inner Unity of the *De Potentia,"Modern Schoolman,* vol. 25 (Jan. 1948), pp. 91-106.

77. *Sum. Theol.,* prologue and I, q. 1, a. 7.

78. Part I of the *Summa Theologiae* contains 119 questions, 584 articles; I-II contains 114 questions, 619 articles; II-II contains 189 questions, 892 articles; III contains 90 questions, 549 articles.

Thomas Aquinas was unable to complete Part III of the *Summa.*

The section that has been published as a Supplement to the *Summa* was a compilation by others (perhaps by Reginald of Piperno) of passages from the *Commentary on the Sentences.* See I. T. Eschmann, O.P., *A Catalogue of St. Thomas' Works* in Etienne Gilson, *The Christian Philosophy of St. Thomas Aquinas* (New York: Random House, 1956), pp. 386-388.

79. Martin Grabmann, *The Interior Life of St. Thomas Aquinas,* tr. by Nicholas Ashenbrenner (Milwaukee: Bruce, 1951), p. 7, from *Responsio de articulis XXXVI ad lectorem Venetum* (1271); see J. Destrez, "La lettre de S. Thomas d'Aquin dite lettre au lecteur de Venise, d'après la traduction manuscrite," *Mélanges Mandonnet* (Paris, 1930), pp. 103-189.

80. See Bourke, *op. cit.,* p. 149 and Thomas Aquinas, *Responsio ad fr. Joannem Vercellensem de articulis XLII,* in Mandonnet, *Opuscula Omnia* III, p. 196 and *Opus. Theol.* (Turin: Marietti, 1954), I, pp. 211-218.

81. See Eschmann, *A Catalogue of St. Thomas' Works,* in Gilson, *The Christian Philosophy of St. Thomas Aquinas,* pp. 384-430; Weisheipl, *A Brief Catalogue of Authentic Works,* in *op. cit.,* pp. 355-405.

82. Aristotle, *On the Soul,* II, c. 1 & 2, in McKeon, *op. cit.,* pp. 554-559.

83. *Sum. Theol.* I, q. 75, a. 1; q. 76, a. 1 & a. 4; *Quaestiones de Anima,* ed. James H. Robb (Toronto: Pontifical Institute of Medieval Studies, 1968), q. 1.

84. *Sum. Theol.* I, q. 75, a. 2. In *Ibid.,* ad 3, he points out that "the body is necessary for the action of the intellect, not as its organ of action but on the part of the object . . . ."

85. Among the thinkers who found the Thomistic position puzzling were Siger of Brabant, John of Jandun, Pietro Pomponazzi. For a discussion of this, see A. C. Pegis, "Some Reflections on *Summa contra Gentiles* II, 56," in *An Etienne Gilson Tribute,* ed. Charles J. O'Neil (Milwaukee: Marquette University Press, 1959), pp. 169-177.

86. *De Unitate Intellectus, tr. cit.,* c. 1, #28, 30, 37-38; c. 3, #84; also *De Spiritualibus Creaturis,* tr. by Mary C. Fitzpatrick & John J. Wellmuth, S.J. (Milwaukee: Marquette University Press, 1949), a. 2.

87. A. C. Pegis, Introduction to *Introduction to Saint Thomas Aquinas* (New York: Modern Library, 1948), p. xxii.

88. *Ibid.,* pp. xxii-xxiii; A. C. Pegis, "St. Thomas and the Unity of Man," in *Progress in Philosophy,* ed. by J. A. McWilliams (Milwaukee: Bruce, 1955), pp. 164-171; Thomas Aquinas, *Sum. Theol.* I, q. 89, a. 1; *Q. D. de Anima,* q. 1.

89. *De Spiritualibus Creaturis,* a. 1.

90. *De Ver.,* q. 8, a. 15; *Cont. Gent.* II, c. 91; *In I Sent.,* dist. 3, q. 4, a. 1, ad 4; *In II Sent.,* dist. 3, q. 1, a. 6.

91. *Sum. Theol.* I, q. 55, a. 2; q. 57, a. 2; q. 85, a. 5.

92. *In II Sent.,* dist. 3, q. 1, a. 6; "Item ex eodem sequuntur aliae differentiae, rationale et intellectuale: quia ex hoc quod angelus plus habet de actu quam anima, et minus habet de potentia, participat quasi in plena luce naturam intellectualem, unde intellectualis dicitur; anima vero, quia extremum gradum in intellectualibus tenet, participat naturam intellectualem magis defective quasi obumbrata; et ideo dicitur rationalis, quia ratio, ut dicit Isaac, in lib. de definit., oritur in umbra intelligentiae."

93. *Sum. Theol.* I, q. 58, a. 3; q. 79, a. 12; *In II Sent.,* dist. 3, q. 1, a. 2; dist. 23, q. 2, a. 1, ad 3.

94. *Sum. Theol.* I, q. 10, a. 1; q. 58, a. 4; *Cont. Gent. II, c. 90;
De Ver.* q. 8, a. 4, ad 15; a. 9; a. 15. On angelic and
human knowledge, see J. Peghaire, *Ratio et Intellectus selon
S. Thomas d'Aquin* (Paris: Vrin; Ottawa: Inst. d'études
médiévales, 1936), esp. parts I & III.

95. *Sum. Theol.* I, q. 62, a. 5, ad 1: "Man, according to his
nature, was not intended to secure his ultimate perfection at once, like the angel. Hence a longer way was
given to man than to the angel for securing beatitude."
See A. C. Pegis, "St. Thomas and the Unity of Man," in
McWilliams, *op. cit.,* p. 172.

96. Aristotle, *Nicomachean Ethics* I, c. 7, 1098a 23 in McKeon,
op. cit., p. 943. Thomas Aquinas in his *Commentary on
Aristotle's Nicomachean Ethics* I, lect. 11 (Paris: Vivès, 1889),
vol. 25, says that time is "quasi adinventor vel bonus
coopertor." He adds: "The meaning is not that time itself
contributes anything but that this help comes with time.
If someone should busy himself investigating the truth
for a period, he will be aided in the discovery of truth by
the passage of time." See Armand Maurer, C.S.B.,
"Time and the Person," in *Proceedings of the American
Catholic Philosophical Association,* vol. LIII (1979), p. 189;
and A. Maurer, *St. Thomas and Historicity* (Milwaukee:
Marquette University Press, 1979), pp. 32-33.

97. Pegis, "Some Permanent Contributions of Medieval
Philosophy to the Notion of Man," in *Transactions of the
Royal Society of Canada,* Third Series, Section II, vol. 46
(1952), p. 73.

98. *Sum. Theol.* I, q. 85, a. 1, resp. & ad 1; a. 2, ad 2.

99. *De Spirit. Creatur.,* a. 2.

100. *Sum. Theol.* I, q. 85, a. 4, ad 1; q. 112, a. 1, ad 1; I-II, q.
53, a. 3, ad 3; q. 113, a. 7, ad 5; *Cont. Gent.* III, c. 61.

101. *In II Sent.,* dist. 3, q. 1, a. 6, dist. 39, q. 3, a. 1.

102. *Sum. Theol.* I, q. 77, a. 2; *Cont. Gent.* II, c. 68; IV, c. 55.
See Jean Mouroux, *The Meaning of Man* (New York:
Sheed & Ward, 1948), pp. 115-117.

103. *Cont. Gent.* II, c. 81.

104. *De Ver.,* q. 18, a. 6; *Sum. Theol.* I-II, q. 2, a. 8; q. 1, a. 4; *Cont. Gent.* I, c. 4.

105. John Godfrey Saxe, "The Blind Men and the Elephant," in Burton E. Stevenson, ed., *The Home Book of Verse for Young Folks,* pp. 180-182.

106. Plato, *Republic* VI, 486 in B. Jowett, *op. cit.,* vol. 1, p. 747.

107. *In II Met.,* lect. 1, #287-288; *In XII Met.,* lect 9, #2566.

108. *Sum. Theol.* I-II, q. 109, a. 1, ad 1.

109. *Compendium Theologiae* (Rome, Leonine ed., 1949), vol. 42, c. 104 & 106; *Sum. Theol.* I-II, q. 3, a. 8; *Cont. Gent.* I, c. 4; III, c. 25 & c. 37 & c. 63.

110. *Cont. Gent.* I, c. 2.

111. *Ibid.,* III, c. 48 & c. 63.

112. Epicurus, "Letter to Menoeceus," in *Epicurus: The Extant Remains,* tr. by Cyril Bailey (Oxford: Clarendon Press, 1926), p. 83.

Published by the Marquette University Press
Milwaukee, Wisconsin 53233
United States of America

#1 St. Thomas and the Life of Learning (1937)
by John F. McCormick, S.J. (1874-1943)
professor of philosophy, Loyola University.
ISBN 0-87462-101-1

#2 St. Thomas and the Gentiles (1938) by Mortimer J. Adler, Ph.D., Director of the Institute of Philosophical Research, San Francisco, Calif.   ISBN 0-87462-102-X

#3 St. Thomas and the Greeks (1939) by Anton C. Pegis, Ph.D., professor of philosophy, Pontifical Institute of Mediaeval Studies, Toronto.   ISBN 0-87462-103-8

#4 The Nature and Functions of Authority (1940) by Yves Simon, Ph.D., (1903-1961) professor of philosophy of social thought, University of Chicago.   ISBN 0-87462-104-6

#5 St. Thomas and Analogy (1941) by Gerald B. Phelan, Ph.D., (1892-1965) professor of philosophy, St. Michael's College, Toronto.
ISBN 0-87462-105-4

#6 St. Thomas and the Problem of Evil (1942) by Jacques Maritain, Ph.D., professor *emeritus* of philosophy, Princeton University.
ISBN 0-87462-106-2

#7 Humanism and Theology (1943) by Werner Jaeger, Ph.D., Litt.D., (1888-1961) University professor, Harvard University.
ISBN 0-87462-107-0

#8 The Nature and Origins of Scientism (1944) by John Wellmuth, Chairman of the Department of Philosophy, Loyola University.
ISBN 0-87462-108-9

#9 Cicero in the Courtroom of St. Thomas Aquinas (1945) by E. K. Rand, Ph.D., Litt D., LL.D. (1871-1945) Pope professor of Latin, *emeritus,* Harvard University. ISBN 0-87462-109-7

#10 St. Thomas and Epistemology (1946) by Louis-Marie Regis, O.P., Th.L., Ph.D., director of the Albert the Great Institute of Mediaeval Studies, University of Montreal.
ISBN 0-87462-110-0

#11 St. Thomas and the Greek Moralists (1947, Spring) by Vernon J. Bourke, Ph.D., professor of philosophy, St. Louis University, St. Louis, Missouri. ISBN 0-87462-111-9

#12 History of Philosophy and Philosophical Education (1947, Fall) by Etienne Gilson of the *Académie français,* director of studies and professor of the history of Mediaeval philosophy, Pontifical Institute of Mediaeval Studies, Toronto. ISBN 0-87462-112-7

#13 The Natural Desire for God (1948) by William R. O'Connor, S.T.L., Ph.D., former professor of dogmatic theology, St. Joseph's Seminary, Dunwoodie, N.Y. ISBN 0-87462-113-5

#14 St. Thomas and the World State (1949) by Robert M. Hutchins, former Chancellor of the University of Chicago, president, of the Fund for the Republic. ISBN 0-87462-114-3

#15 Method in Metaphysics (1950) by Robert J. Henle, S.J., Ph.D., academic vice-president, St. Louis University, St. Louis, Missouri.
ISBN 0-87462-115-1

#16 Wisdom and Love in St. Thomas Aquinas (1951) by Etienne Gilson of the *Académie français*, director of studies and professor of the history of Mediaeval philosophy, Pontifical Institute of Mediaeval Studies, Toronto.
ISBN 0-87462-116-X

#17 The Good in Existential Metaphysics (1952) by Elizabeth G. Salmon, Ph.D., professor of philosophy in the graduate school, Fordham University.
ISBN 0-87462-117-8

#18 St. Thomas and the Object of Geometry (1953) by Vincent Edward Smith, Ph.D., director, Philosophy of Science Institute, St. John's University.
ISBN 0-87462-118-6

#19 Realism and Nominalism Revisited (1954) by Henry Veatch, Ph.D., professor and chairman of the department of philosophy, Northwestern University.
ISBN 0-87462-119-4

#20 Imprudence in St. Thomas Aquinas (1955) by Charles J. O'Neil, Ph.D., professor of philosophy, Villanova University.
ISBN 0-87462-120-8

#21 The Truth That Frees (1956) by Gerard Smith, S.J., Ph.D., professor of philosophy, Marquette University.
ISBN 0-87462-121-6

#22 St. Thomas and the Future of Metaphysics (1957) by Joseph Owens, C.Ss.R., Ph.D., professor of philosophy, Pontifical Institute of Mediaeval Studies, Toronto.
ISBN 0-87462-122-4

#23 Thomas and the Physics of 1958: A Confrontation (1958) by Henry Margenau, Ph.D., Eugene Higgins professor of physics and natural philosophy, Yale University.
ISBN 0-87462-123-2

#24 Metaphysics and Ideology (1959) by Wm. Oliver Martin, Ph.D., professor of philosophy, University of Rhode Island.
ISBN 0-87462-124-0

#25 Language, Truth and Poetry (1960) by Victor M. Hamm, Ph.D., professor of English, Marquette University.   ISBN 0-87462-125-9

#26 Metaphysics and Historicity (1961) by Emil L. Fackenheim, Ph.D., professor of philosophy, University of Toronto.
ISBN 0-87462-126-7

#27 The Lure of Wisdom (1962) by James D. Collins, Ph.D., professor of philosophy, St. Louis University.   ISBN 0-87462-127-5

#28 Religion and Art (1963) by Paul Weiss, Ph.D. Sterling professor of philosophy, Yale University.   ISBN 0-87462-128-3

#29 St. Thomas and Philosophy (1964) by Anton C. Pegis, Ph.D., professor of philosophy, Pontifical Institute of Mediaeval Studies, Toronto.   ISBN 0-87462-129-1

#30 The University in Process (1965) by John O. Riedl, Ph.D., dean of faculty, Queensboro Community College.   ISBN 0-87462-130-5

#31 The Pragmatic Meaning of God (1966) by Robert O. Johann, associate professor of philosophy, Fordham University.
ISBN 0-87462-131-3

#32 Religion and Empiricism (1967) by John E. Smith, Ph.D., professor of philosophy, Yale University.   ISBN 0-87462-132-1

#33 The Subject (1968) by Bernard Lonergan, S.J., S.T.D., professor of dogmatic theory, Regis College, Ontario and Gregorian University, Rome. ISBN 0-87462-133-X

#34 Beyond Trinity (1969) by Bernard J. Cooke, S.J., S.T.D., Marquette University.
ISBN 0-87462-134-8

#35 Ideas and Concepts (1970) by Julius R. Weinberg, Ph.D., (1908-1971) Vilas Professor of Philosophy, University of Wisconsin.
ISBN 0-87462-135-6

#36 Reason and Faith Revisited (1971) by Francis H. Parker, Ph.D., head of the philosophy department, Purdue University, Lafayette, Indiana. ISBN 0-87462-136-4

#37 Psyche and Cerebrum (1972) by John N. Findlay, M.A. Oxon, Ph.D., Clark Professor of Moral Philosophy and Metaphysics, Yale University. ISBN 0-87462-137-2

#38 The Problem of the Criterion (1973) by Roderick M. Chisholm, Ph.D., Andrew W. Mellon, Professor in the Humanities, Brown University. ISBN 0-87462-138-0

#39 Man as Infinite Spirit (1974) by James H. Robb, Ph.D., professor of philosophy, Marquette University. ISBN 0-87462-139-9

#40 Aquinas to Whitehead: Seven Centuries of Metaphysics of Religion (1976) by Charles E. Hartshorne, Ph.D., professor of philosophy, the University of Texas at Austin.
ISBN 0-87462-141-0

#41 The Problem of Evil (1977) by Errol E. Harris, D.Litt., Distinguished Visiting Professor of Philosophy, Marquette University.
ISBN 0-87462-142-9

#42 The Catholic University and the Faith (1978) by Francis C. Wade, S.J., professor of philosophy, Marquette University.
ISBN 0-87462-143-7

#43 St. Thomas and Historicity (1979) by Armand Maurer, C.S.B., professor of philosophy, University of Toronto and the Pontifical Institute of Mediaeval Studies, Toronto.
ISBN 0-87462-144-5

#44 Does God Have a Nature? (1980) by Alvin Plantinga, Ph.D., professor of philosophy, Calvin College, Grand Rapids, Michigan.
ISBN 0-87462-145-3

#45 Rhyme and Reason: St. Thomas and Modes of Discourse (1981) by Ralph McInerny, Ph.D., professor of Medieval Studies, University of Notre Dame.
ISBN 0-87462-148-8

#46 The Gift: Creation (1982) by Kenneth L. Schmitz, Ph.D., professor of philosophy at Trinity College, University of Toronto.
ISBN 0-87462-149-6

#47 How Philosophy Begins (1983) by Beatrice H. Zedler, Ph.D., Professor of Philosophy at Marquette University.
ISBN 0-87462-151-8

Uniform format, cover and binding.

Copies of this Aquinas Lecture and the others in the series are obtainable from:

Marquette University Press
Marquette University
Milwaukee, Wisconsin 53233, U.S.A.

Publishers of:

- Mediaeval Philosophical Texts in Translations
- Père Marquette Theology Lectures
- St. Thomas Aquinas Lectures